ATHANASIANA SYRIACA

PART II

1. HOMILY ON MATTHEW XII 32 (Epistola ad Serapionem IV § 8-23). 2. EPISTOLA AD AFROS. 3. TOMUS AD ANTIOCHENOS. 4. EPISTOLA AD MAXIMUM. 5. EPISTOLA AD ADELPHIUM

CORPUS

SCRIPTORUM CHRISTIANORUM ORIENTALIUM

EDITUM CONSILIO

UNIVERSITATIS CATHOLICAE AMERICAE

ET UNIVERSITATIS CATHOLICAE LOVANIENSIS

Vol. 273

SCRIPTORES SYRI

TOMUS 119

ATHANASIANA SYRIACA

PART II

1. HOMILY ON MATTHEW XII 32 (Epistola ad Serapionem IV § 8-32. 2. EPISTOLA AD AFROS. 3. TOMUS AD ANTIOCHENOS. 4. EPISTOLA AD MAXIMUM. 5. EPISTOLA AD ADELPHIUM

TRANSLATED

BY

ROBERT W. THOMSON

LOVANII

IN AEDIBUS E. PEETERS

1967

CORPUS
SCRIPTORUM CHRISTIANORUM ORIENTALIUM

EDITUM CONSILIO

UNIVERSITATIS CATHOLICAE AMERICAE
ET UNIVERSITATIS CATHOLICAE LOVANIENSIS

Vol. 273

SCRIPTORES SYRI

TOMUS 119

ATHANASIANA SYRIACA

PART II

1. HOMILY ON MATTHEW XII 32 (Epistola ad Serapionem IV § 8-23). 2. EPISTOLA AD AFROS. 3. TOMUS AD ANTIOCHENOS. 4. EPISTOLA AD MAXIMUM. 5. EPISTOLA AD ADELPHIUM

TRANSLATED

BY

ROBERT W. THOMSON

LOUVAIN
SECRÉTARIAT DU CorpusSCO
49, CH. DE WAVRE
1967

INTRODUCTION

This is the second volume of translations of the Syriac versions of dogmatic works by St. Athanasius. The first four of the texts here translated (*Ad Serapionem IV* §8-23, *Ad Afros*, *Ad Antiochenos* and *Ad Maximum*) have survived only in one manuscript, British Museum Or. 8606, dated to 723 A.D., which is of particular interest as it contains the only known collection of *Athanasiana syriaca* (for details see the Introduction to the volume of texts). The *Ad Adelphium* is found in both this manuscript and British Museum Add. 14531 of the seventh or eighth century; the two texts are slightly corrupted copies of the same translation.

As before, the references to Old Testament quotations follow the Septuagint numbering. The translations and the Syriac texts have been divided into sections corresponding to those of the Greek edition in J.P. Migne's *Patrologia Graeca* vol. 26. (The *Ad Serapionem IV* § 8-23 is printed on col. 648-676, *the Ad Afros* on col. 1029-1048, the *Ad Antiochenos* on col. 796-809, the *Ad Maximum* on col. 1085-1089 and the *Ad Adelphium* on col. 1072-1084).

DISCOURSE OF THE SAME SAINT ATHANASIUS, BISHOP, ON THE SAYING IN THE GOSPEL : « WHOEVER BLASPHEMES AGAINST THE SPIRIT WILL NOT BE FORGIVEN ».

8 Concerning the saying in the gospel to which you referred when
5 writing to me, forgive me my friend, as you are well disposed towards me, for I have been for some time afraid to tackle it, lest becoming involved in the profundity of this question and beginning to enquire into it, I be unable to draw out the full significance contained in it. So I wished to remain completely silent and to be content merely
10 with what had been written previously. But I took thought, in case you should write a second time and seek from me an explanation of the saying, and forced myself to impart to you what little understanding I have of it, trusting that if I attain its meaning you will receive it on account of Him who enjoined it, but
15 that if I fail I shall not be blamed by you since you know our diligence and weakness.

The saying is this. When the Pharisees saw all the signs done by our Lord which are mentioned in the holy gospel, they said : « This man does not cast out demons save by Beelzebub chief of the
20 demons ». But our Lord knew their thoughts and said to them : « Every kingdom which is divided against itself will perish ». And He said : « If I cast out demons by the Spirit of God, the kingdom of God has come upon you [1] ». And then He added : « Therefore I say to you that all sins and blasphemies will be forgiven you men,
25 but blasphemy against the holy Spirit * will not be forgiven you,   * 2 p. neither in this world nor in the world to come [2] ». And you were wondering why blasphemy against the Son would be forgiven, but blasphemy against the holy Spirit would not be forgiven, neither in this world nor in the world to come.

[1] Cf. *Mt.*, 12, 24-28.   [2] Cf. *Mt.*, 12, 31-32.

9 So former men, the very learned and industrious Origen and
the amazing and diligent Theognostus (for I saw their discourses
on this when you wrote your letter to me), both wrote that this
is the blasphemy against the holy Spirit, saying that when a man
⁵ through baptism has become worthy of the gift of the holy Spirit
and turns back to do sin, he has no forgiveness. As Paul said in
the letter to the Hebrews : « Those who have once gone down to
baptism, and have tasted of the gift from heaven and have received
the holy Spirit and have tasted the good word of God and the power
¹⁰ of the world to come, and may sin again, cannot be renewed to
repentance ¹». They both alike say this, and singly also add their
opinion.

10 For Origen says that the cause of the judgement against
the blasphemers is this : that God and the Father is in all and
¹⁵ contains all, inanimate and animate, rational and irrational; but
the power of the Son extends only to rational (creatures), among
which are the catechumens and the heathen who have not believed;
and the holy Spirit is only in those who receive Him through the
gift of baptism. So when the catechumens and the heathen sin,
²⁰ they sin against the Son, for He is in them, as was said; and they
are able to gain forgiveness when they become worthy of the gift
through rebirth. And when those who have been baptised sin,
they sin against the holy Spirit because they sinned after they
were in Him, and there is no pardon for the judgement against
²⁵ them ².

* **11** But Theognostus added the following arguments. Whoever * p. 3
transgresses the first or second limit is judged less; but ⌐whoever
(passes) the third ³ has no pardon. The first and second are said of
the Father and the Son, but the third of the holy Spirit. And wishing
³⁰ to complete his remark, he mentioned the saying of our Saviour
to his disciples : « I still have much to say to you, but you are not
able to receive it. But when the holy Spirit comes. He will teach
you ⁴». So these things our Saviour said to those who are not able
to receive them completely, submitting to their weakness. But
³⁵ those who have been perfected become receivers of the holy Spirit,

---

¹ *Heb.*, 6, 4-6.   ² Origen *De Principiis* I 3, 5.   ³ *Syr* : the third judgement.
⁴ *Jn.*, 16, 12-13.

yet do not exceed the teaching of the Son; but the Son condescends
to those who are not perfect, and the holy Spirit is the seal for
those who have been made perfect. And such [1] is the blasphemy
against the holy Spirit. Not because the Spirit surpasses the Son,
5 but because those who have not been perfected have pardon, but
to those who are perfected and have tasted of the gift from heaven,
not one pardon remains. Such are their arguments.

12 But from what I have learned, I think that the opinion of
each one of them is lacking in investigation, and we must see if
10 there be not a more hidden and profounder meaning in it. For it is
clear that what the Father is the Son is also, and what the Father
and the Son are the holy Spirit is also, for the holy Trinity is
without distinction and perfect. And again, if everything came into
being by the Son [2] and everything exists in Him [3], how would He
15 be outside what had been made by Him? So since they are not
without Him, whoever sins against the Son and blasphemes necessarily
also sins against the Father and the holy Spirit. If holy baptism was
given only in the Spirit, one could say that those who had been
baptised * and then sinned, sinned only against the Spirit; but since   * p. 4
20 baptism is given in the Father and in the Son and in the holy Spirit,
and everyone who is baptised is made perfect in this way, if they
fall into blasphemy after baptism they necessarily blaspheme against
the holy and indivisible Trinity.

And again we must consider and reflect on this : that if our
25 Lord had said these things after the Pharisees had accepted baptism
and had previously received the gift of the holy Spirit, this opinion
would be acceptable in that they had turned and sinned against the
holy Spirit. But if they had not accepted baptism but had despised
even John's baptism, how would He have blamed them for blas-
30 pheming against the holy Spirit of whom they had never partaken?
For our Lord did not say these things simply to teach us, but our
Lord made this remark adducing the rebukes of this judgement
and truly blaming the Pharisees, who were already under the
judgement of this great blasphemy. So since the Pharisees were
35 accused of this even before they received baptism, it is clear that

---

[1] *Syr* : now (sic !)   [2] Cf. *Jn.*, *1, 3.*   [3] *Coloss.*, *1, 17.*

this saying does not concern those who have transgressed after baptism; for He did not find fault with them simply because of (their) sins, but He brought this charge upon them because of blasphemy. And there is a difference here, for the one transgresses
5 the law, and the one who blasphemes acts impiously against the Godhead Himself. So since they had been blamed previously by our Saviour for many things - for transgressing the commandment of God [1] concerning their parents, and for their love of money, and for abandoning the sayings of the prophets, and for making the
10 house of God a house of commerce - He warned them to repent. And when they said that He cast out devils by Beelzebub, He showed that this was not merely a sin but blasphemy, from which those who dared to say such things could neither escape nor have pardon at the judgement.

15 **13** But if this saying about blasphemy was expressed for the sake of those who sin after baptism, how could the Apostle write to the Corinthians concerning him who sinned in Corinth * that they   * p . 5 should receive him again in love [2], or again say to the Galatians who had backslided after baptism : « My children whom I again travail
20 until Christ be again depicted in you [3] » ? And in saying « again » he demonstrated their former perfection in the Spirit. Why then do we also blame him who said that there is no repentance after baptism, if this saying was directed to those who sin after baptism ? For the Apostle did not exclude (such) from repentance when he
25 said this to the Hebrews. Far from it ! But he showed that there is only one perfection through it and not two. For he wrote thus to the Hebrews lest they should suppose that there are frequent baptisms every day for the sake of repentance according to the custom of of the law [4]. And he urged them to repent, showing that there is
30 only one and not two renewals, as again in another letter he writes : « One faith and one baptism [5] ». For he did not say that it was impossible to repent, but that it was impossible after baptism to renew another baptism. And there is here a geat difference, for he who repents desists from sin, but he has the scars of the sores; but
35 he who is baptised strips off the old man, and is renewed and is born as it were again through the grace of the holy Spirit.

---

[1] *Syr. add* and (sic !)   [2] Cf. II *Cor.*, 2, 8.   [3] *Galat.*, 4, 19.   [4] Cf. *Heb.*, 9, 10.
[5] *Eph.*, 4, 5.

14 So having these thoughts, I considered that there was a greater depth of meaning in this saying; and therefore after many petitions to the Lord who sat at the well and walked on the waters of the sea, I now progress to the dispensation effected on our behalf
5 in Him, that I may perhaps be able through my reading to draw out its meaning. Now all the divine Scriptures announce and preach this dispensation, and especially John by saying : « The Word became flesh and dwelt among us [1] ». And again Paul writes : « Being in the form of God, * He thought it no violation to be equal * p. 6
10 to God, but emptied Himself and took the form of a servant and was found in appearance as a man; and He humbled Himself and was obedient to death, even the death of the cross [2] ». So since He is God and became man, as God He raised the dead and by a word healed everyone; He also changed water into wine, and these
15 were not the works of a man. And because He had put on a body, He was thirsty and toiled and suffered; and these are not (the marks) of divinity. And as God He said : « I am in my Father and my Father in me [3] »; and as having a body He reprimanded the Jews, saying : « Why do you wish to kill me, a man who spoke
20 the truth to you, what I have heard from the Father [4] ? » And these things were done not separately according to their kind, but all were performed together. Yet there is one Lord who performed them by his grace; for the divine (works) were not done without the body, nor the bodily without the divinity. So He spat bodily,
25 and it was divine, for by it He opened the eyes of the blind man. And wishing to show that He was God, with a bodily tongue He said : « I and my Father are one [5] »; and merely by his will He healed everyone. For He stretched out a bodily hand and raised Simon's mother-in-law from a fever, and also the daughter of the head of
30 the synagogue from the dead.

15 So of the heretics who have been perverted by their ignorance, some seeing the bodily nature of our Lord and Saviour denied that : « In the beginning was the Word [6] »; and others seeing his divinity did not recognise that : « The Word became flesh and
35 dwelt among us [7] ». But the faithful and apostolic man, conversant with the loving kindness of God and seeing the marvels of the

---

[1] *Jn.*, 1, *14.*   [2] *Philipp.*, 2, *6-8.*   [3] *Jn.*, 14, *11.*   [4] *Jn.*, 8, *40.*   [5] *Jn.*,
10, *30.*   [6] *Jn.*, 1, *1.*   [7] *Jn.*, 1, *14.*

divinity, wondered at the Lord in a body; and again considering
the characteristics of the body, he wondered at the activity through
them of the divinity. And since this is * the faith in the holy church,   * p. 7
if men consider the bodily aspects and see our Lord hungry and
5 thirsty and suffering, and only speak superfluities about our Saviour
as of a man, then they sin greatly; but they can obtain pardon
if they immediately repent, having an excuse in the weakness
of the body. And again, when they consider the deeds of the divinity
and hesitate in human fashion about the nature of the body, they
10 also sin greatly, since, although they saw our Lord eating and
suffering, they have slipped into phantasies. Yet the Word is able
to pardon them, since they have an excuse in the sight of the super-
human greatness of the deeds. But when those who are supposed
to have a knowledge of the law, that is the Pharisees, surpass in
15 their blindness the ignorance of these men, and turn in anger and
completely deny the Word in the flesh, or ascribe the deeds of the
divinity to the devil and his ministers, they have no pardon in the
judgement which comes upon them from this impiety, for they
considered the devil to be God, and thought that He who is truly
20 God had nothing superior in his works to the demons.

16 Now into this impiety had fallen the Jews, and more than
the Jews the Pharisees. For when our Saviour was demonstrating
the works of the Father, raising the dead, opening (the eyes of)
the blind, making the lame to walk, the deaf to hear and the mute
25 to speak, and showing creation subject to Himself, rebuking the
wind and walking on the sea, and crowds were amazed and praised
God, then the Pharisees said that these deeds were Beelzebub's,
and in their folly were not ashamed to ascribe the works of God to
the devil. And therefore our Saviour indicated that there is no
30 pardon for this blasphemy of theirs. For while they saw the human
deeds (of Christ) and their mind was crippled and they said : « Is not
He the son of the carpenter ? [1]» * and : « How does He know letters   * p. 8
when He has not studied ? [2]» and : « What sign have you made concerning yourself ? [3]» and : « Let Him come down now from the cross
35 and we shall believe in Him [4]», He endured them as sinning against
the son of man. And being weary He said to them : « If you knew

---

[1] *Mt.*, 13, 55.   [2] *Jn.*, 7, 15.   [3] *Jn.*, 6 30.   [4] *Mt.*, 27, 42.

the things of peace [1].» And Peter, when the maid spoke with him
and he so replied as a man, our Lord forgave when he wept and fell.
These Pharisees were so stirred up as to say that the works of
God were of Beelzebub, and since they went so far in their audacity
5 He condemned them with an eternal judgement. For it was the same
for them as to dare to say, seeing the order of creation and the
providence (of God) in it, that it came into being by Beelzebub,
and the sun rises in obedience to the devil and the stars circle in
the firmament by him. For if these are the wonders of God, so
10 those are the works of the Father; and if those are the works of
Beelzebub, so these must be signs of Beelzebub according to their [2]
reasoning. And what is their source for : « In the beginning God
made heaven and earth [3] » ?

Yet this confusion is not foreign to them, because the originators
15 of this opinion of theirs shortly after going out of Egypt
made themselves a calf, and the blessings that came from God
they attributed to it, saying : « These are your gods who brought
you out of the land of Egypt [4] ». So on that account many who
dared (to utter) this blasphemy perished at that time. And God
20 said : « When I try them, I shall bring upon them their sins [5] ».
For when they clamoured for bread and water He endured them
as a nurse endures her child, but when they became more disor-
derly, as the Spirit of God sings against them : « They changed
their glory * into the form of an ox that eats grass [6]», then because * p. 9
25 of their great audacity they were destroyed, as it is written in the
Scripture concerning the calf which Aaron made.

17 Such then is the daring of the Pharisees and such the punishment they received from our Saviour, that they also should go to
the fire which is prepared and with him (Beelzebub) be judged in
30 it for ever. This was declared by our Lord and Saviour Jesus Christ,
not as if the Spirit was greater than He and therefore the accusation
against the Spirit was greater. Far from it ! For He anticipated
this and taught that everything the Father has the Son has also,
and the Spirit receives from the Son and glorifies the Son. The
35 Spirit does not give the Son, but the Son gives the Spirit to his
disciples, and through them to those who believe in Him.

---

[1] *Lk.*, 19, 42.   [2] *Syr* : your (sic !).   [3] *Gen.*, 1, 1.   [4] *Ex.*, 32, 4.   [5] *Ex.*, 32, 4.
[6] *Ps.*, 105, 20.

So if our Saviour spoke thus, it is clear that all the blasphemy was against Him and that one blasphemy was greater and one lesser. For the Pharisees spoke both : seeing Him as a man they slandered Him : « Whence has this man this wisdom [1] ? » and :
[5] « You are not fifty years old and have seen Abraham [2] ? » and seeing the works of the Father, they did not only deny his divinity, but instead said that Beelzebub was in Him and that these were his works. Therefore, as the blasphemy was spoken against Him, the lesser concerning his manhood, the greater concerning his
[10] divinity, it was on account of the greater that the punishment of this judgement came upon them, from which they will never escape. For when He strengthened his disciples He said to them : « If they called the lord of the house Beelzebub [3] », showing Himself to be the lord of the house, and that is was He who was being blasphemed
[15] by the Jews.

18 It is clear that the whole saying « the blasphemy against the Spirit » is meant of our Saviour, for when He said this He showed that He is * the lord of the house of the universe; and I do   * p. 10 not shrink from repeating these remarks for the sake of certainty.
[20] To thirst, to toil, to sleep, to be tempted, to eat are (properties) of a man; but the works which our Lord effected were not a man's to do but God's. So when, as I said above, they saw these things and reviled our Lord as a man, they received a lesser punishment than those who attributed the works of God to the devil. For such people
[25] not only gave what is holy to the dogs, but equated the devil with God and said that light was darkness and darkness light. This is the unpardonable blasphemy for the Pharisees, and it was this that the Evangelist Mark clearly demonstrated when he said : « Whoever blasphemes against the holy Spirit has no forgiveness but is con-
[30] demned to eternal judgement, because they said : 'He has an impure Spirit' [4] ». For the man blind from his mother's womb, when (his eyes) were opened and he saw the light, also bore witness and said : « Never has it been heard that a man opened the eyes of a man born blind; unless he was from God he would not have been
[35] able to do this [5] ». And the crowds, when they heard what was being

---

[1] *Mt.,* 13, 54.   [2] *Jn.,* 8, 57.   [3] *Mt.,* 10, 25.   [4] *Mk.,* 3, 29-30.   [5] *Jn.,* 9, 32-33.

said by our Lord, declared : « These words are not of one who has
a demon, for a demon cannot open the eyes of a blind man [1] ».

But the Pharisees who were considered to be versed in the law,
who widened the fringes of their mantles and boasted of knowing
5 more than other men, were not ashamed, but as is written, in their
weakness sacrificed to demons and not to God [2], and said that our
Lord had a devil and that the works of God were a devil's. And
this they did only to deny completely that He who worked these
things was God and the Son of God. For if the fact that He ate
10 and his bodily appearance * showed Him to be a man, why from   * p. 11
his works did they not grasp that He was in the Father and the
Father in Him ? But they did not wish to do so, for they had in
themselves Beelzebub, and he was uttering these blasphemies through
them, so that from the works of men they considered our Lord to
15 be merely a man, but from the works of God they did not admit
that He was God ; but they made Beelzebub who was in themselves
God instead of Him, so that they might have their judgement
with Beelzebub in eternal fire.

19 So this is the careful examination of the reading of this
20 book, and it shows that both blasphemies affect Him and (that)
concerning Himself He spoke of the blasphemy against the son
of man and the Spirit, to show thereby his bodily nature, and by
the Spirit to demonstrate his spiritual existence and renown and
divinity. For what can obtain forgiveness He posited concerning
25 his humanity, but the blasphemy which cannot be forgiven He
showed to be spoken against the Spirit, as He also thereby declared
his divinity. And this sense He also showed in the gospel of John :
when He was speaking about the nourishment of his body and
saw some offended by it, our Lord said to them : « Does this offend
30 you, if you see the Son of Man ascending to where He was formerly ?
It is the Spirit that gives life ; the body is of no avail. The words
which I spoke with you are Spirit and life [3] ». And here He mentioned
them both concerning Himself, body and Spirit. And He distin-
guished the Spirit from what is in the body, that they might believe
35 and learn, not only from what is visible but also from what is
invisible, that the things He spoke were not bodily but spiritual.

---

[1] *Jn.*, 10, 21.   [2] Cf. *Deut.*, 32, 17.   [3] *Jn.*, 6, 61-63.

For to what extent did the body suffice for food, that it might
be sufficient for the whole world also as food ? But for this reason
He mentioned the ascension of the Son of Man to heaven, to separate
them from corporeal considerations * and that they might thence-   * p. 12
5 forth learn that his body was given by Him as from above and
from heaven and as spiritual (food). « For the words which I spoke
with you are Spirit and life». For what is visible and is given on
behalf of the life of the world is truly that body.

20   For that reason the Son of Man also said that He would be
10 betrayed. For the Word is immortal and intangible and is alive by
his essence. But the Pharisees neither believed these things nor
wished to see what their sons were doing. And therefore our Lord
gently reprimanded them, saying : « If through Beelzebub I cast
out demons, through what do your sons cast them out? And
15 therefore they will be your judges. But if I cast out demons by the
Spirit of God, then the kingdom of God has come upon you [1] ».
And this remark « by the Spirit» He said not as if He were lesser
than the Spirit by whom He worked, but to show again that He is
the Word [2], who is God, and that He did everything through the
20 Spirit, and to teach those who were listening that to the extent
they attributed the work of the Spirit to Beelzebub they were
blaspheming against the giver of the Spirit. By saying [3] this He
showed that not through ignorance but deliberately they had
turned to this blasphemy and become immersed in it. And they
25 were not ashamed, although they knew that these were the works
of God, to attribute them to Beelzebub in their wretchedness,
and to say that they were performed by an unclean spirit.

21   So how can those who have this audacity blame the heathen
for making idols and calling them gods ? For they are equally mad,
30 or perhaps more so in their daring; and although they have received
the law, by transgressing the law they have abused God. But
what will they do, uttering these blasphemies, when they read the
prophet Isaiah and hear from him that these are the signs of the
coming of Christ : the seeing of the blind, * the walking of the lame,   * p. 13
35 the speaking of the dumb, the raising of the dead, the cleansing
of the lepers, the hearing of the deaf? For whom do they wish

---

[1] *Lk.*, 11, *19-20.*   [2] *Syr* : cause (sic !).   [3] *Plural* in *Syr.* (sic !).

to say is the author of these works? If they say He is God they
refute themselves for being impious to our Lord. For what the
prophet foresaw and predicted, our Lord has come and effected
and fulfilled. But if, overcome by arrogance, they say that these
5 were the works of Beelzebub, I tremble lest, gradually increasing
in impiety and reading : « Who gave a mouth to man? And who
made the dumb and the speaking, the blind and the seeing [1]? »
they go mad again and say that these are the words of Beelzebub.
For as he who saw attributed the blessing (of sight) and its absence,
10 the cause of both, to the one God the Word, so by saying these
things they consider that Beelzebub is the controller of human
nature. For it is the characteristic of the maker of something to
have power also over what was made by him. For it is said by
Moses that : « God made heaven and earth [2] », and : « In his image
15 God made man [3] ». And again Daniel boldly said to Cyrus : « I do
not worship idols made by the hands of men, but the living God
who created heaven and earth; and He has power over all flesh [4] ».
I tremble lest the Pharisees turn in their impiety and say that these
chastisements - blindness, lameness and other sufferings - stem
20 from the reproof of the government of the creator, and that their
release and the blessings which come to those suffering from them
are the work of Beelzebub. But if anyone examines this, it is very
stupid [5] and the mark of mad men and people out of their mind in
impiety and senseless talk. For in their weak-mindedness they do
25 not ascribe the comparatively better to God but to Beelzebub.
For they do not hesitate to corrupt the Scriptures and the command-
ments contained therein, merely in order to deny the coming of
Christ.

* **22** The wicked ones ought not to have belittled our Lord for *p. 14
30 his bodily acts, but for his deeds to have confessed that He was
truly God. So they do everything in reverse. When they saw Him
as a man they slandered Him as a man; and when they saw the
works of God they denied his divinity and ran to the devil. And
those who dared to do this thought that they would be able to
35 flee, so that they would not be caught by God the Word who was
being abused by them. The magicians of Pharaoh had previously

[1] *Ex.*, 4, 11.   [2] *Gen.*, 1, 1.   [3] *Gen.*, 1, 27.   [4] *Dan(Bel).*, 14, 5.   [5] *Syr* : vexing.

great daring, but when they saw the wonders done by Moses they
lost their grip and turned away, saying that it was the finger of
God which did them [1]. But the Pharisees and scribes seeing the
whole hand of God working greater and more amazing wonders,
⁵ and seeing that they were done by our Saviour, said that it was
Beelzebub who was doing them [2].

So what greater madness is there than theirs, or what, as the
prophet said, can be compared to their impiety [3]? They have
justified, compared to themselves, the Sodomites and Ninevites and
¹⁰ have overcome in their ignorance even the heathen and surpassed
the folly of the magicians of Pharaoh. They can only be compared
with the Arians, since both groups have fallen into the same impiety.
For the Jews, seeing the works of the Father which were done
by the Son, attributed them to Beelzebub; and the Arians, seeing
¹⁵ the same works, count the Lord who does them with the creatures
and say : « There was a time when He was not », and : « Before He
came into being He was not ». And the Pharisees, seeing our Lord
in the body, murmured saying : « Why since you are a man do you
make yourself God ? [4] » And those who fight with Christ, seeing
²⁰ Him suffering and sleeping, said that He who endures these things
cannot be God of the same nature * as the Father. And if anyone   * p. 15
examined all this, he would find that they had fallen into the same
depth of folly.

23 And therefore our Lord demonstrated that the judgement
²⁵ of the former and the latter cannot be pardoned, saying : « Whoever
speaks against the holy Spirit will not be forgiven, either in this
world or the world to come [5] ». And can perchance whoever denies
the Son, if he makes supplication gain any forgiveness ? Can he
suppose they have life or rest if he rejects Him who said : « I am
³⁰ the life [6] », and : « Come to me, you who are heavily laden, and
I shall give you rest [7] » ? So since they receive such judgement,
it is clear that those who serve Christ and worship his Spirit and
his body, and do not forget that He is the Son of God or deny that
He became man, but believe that : « In the beginning was the
³⁵ Word [8] », and : « The Word became flesh and dwelt among us [9] »,
will reign for ever according to the holy promises of our Lord and

---

[1] Cf. *Ex.*, 8, *19*.   [2] Cf. *Mt.*, 12, *24*; *Lk.*, 11, *15*.   [3] Cf. *Lam.*, 2, *13*.   [4] *Jn.*,
10, *33*.   [5] *Mt.*, 12, *32*.   [6] *Jn.*, 14, *6*.   [7] *Mt.*, 11, *28*.   [8] *Jn.*, 1, *1*.   [9] *Jn.*,1, *14*.

Saviour Himself, who said : « They will go to eternal judgement, and the just to everlasting life [1]».

These brief remarks I have written down from what I have learned, and do you receive them from me not as the complete 5 teaching but as a timely (précis); and take henceforth the tested meaning from the gospel and the psalms, and bind fast the sheaves of the truth. As you carry them men will say : « He comes with joy who bears his sheaf [2] » in Jesus Christ our Lord, to whom with his Father and the holy Spirit be glory for ever and ever. Amen.

10 End of the Discourse of Saint Athanasius of Alexandria.

---

[1] *Mt.*, 25, 46.   [2] Cf. *Ps.*, 125, 6.

1 Enough has been written by our beloved fellow minister Damasus, bishop of great Rome, and by all the bishops who gathered there, and no less suffice the councils held in Gaul and Italy con-
5 cerning the right faith which the Lord bestowed [1], the Apostles preached, and the Fathers handed down when they gathered in Nicaea from the whole of our world. For all this effort was then expended on account of the Arian heresy, so that those who had fallen into it might rise up, and its inventors be revealed. So
10 previously the whole world had followed it; but now after many councils have been held and all those called to remembrance, who in Dalmatia and Dardania and Macedonia and Epirus and Hellas and Crete, and the other islands Sicily and Cyprus, and Pamphylia and Lycia and Isauria, and all Egypt and the Libyas, with the majority
15 of those in Arabia had approved it, then they admired those who signed, that if any of them lacked [2] the bitterness of the root of the Arians which had sprung up, I mean Auxentius and Ursacius and Valentinus and those who shared their opinions, these by their writings were excommunicated and effaced. So what was affirmed
20 at Nicaea is sufficient and adequate, as we said above, for the over- throw of all impious heresies and for the security and profit of the church's teaching.

But because we have heard that some are attempting to combat it, and are daring to entitle « council » such as took place in Ariminum,
25 * and are struggling that the latter prevail over the former,   * p. 17 then we decided that we must write and remind you that you consent not to such things, for it is nothing more than the Arian weed. For those who reject the council which was held to oppose it, that is the one in Nicaea, what else do they wish save the victory
30 of Arius's ideas? And of what are such people worthy save to be called Arians and to share the same punishment as they? They fear not God who said : « Do not alter the ancient boundaries which your fathers set [3] », and : « Who speaks ill of his father or mother

---

[1] *Syr.* : gathered (sic !)   [2] Sic !   [3] *Prov.*, *22*, *28*.

will die by death[1]». And they had no reverence for the Fathers who commanded that those who thought contrary to their confession be anathematised.

2 For this reason the council held at Nicaea was an universal one, three hundred and eighteen bishops gathering for the faith against the Arian impiety, that there might be no more local ones for the sake of the faith, but even if such were held, they should not be definitive. For what does this (council) lack that one should seek new ones? It is complete in piety, beloved; it has filled the whole world. This even the Indians have recognised, and all the Christians among the other barbarians. So vain is the struggle of those who have frequently attempted to oppose it. For behold such people have made some ten councils or more, changing in every one of them, taking away some things from the earlier and altering and adding things in the later ones. They have gained no profit, writing and erasing up to now, using force and being unaware that : « Every plant which my Father in heaven has not planted will be uprooted[2] ». But the word of the Lord fixed at the ecumenical council of Nicaea remains for ever. For if anyone were to compare numbers, *that at Nicaea is greater than those of the local ones to   *p. 18 the same extent that the whole is greater than the parts. And if anyone wished to know the reason for that of Nicaea and for all the councils which were held by them after it, he would find that that of Nicaea had a proper cause, but that those others were forcibly held for reasons of hate and contention. For the one was held on account of the Arian heresy and the question of Easter, because those in Syria and Cilicia and Mesopotamia differed from us and they celebrated it at the same time as the Jews. But thanks be to God, that just as there was agreement on the faith, so there was also on the festival. And this was the cause of the council of Nicaea. But those that were held after it were on behalf of Arius and against the ecumenical council.

3 Since this is the case, who would approve of those who name the council of Ariminum or any other? Or who would not hate those who despise the acts of the Fathers, but honour the recent acts of Ariminum which were composed in contention and by force?

---

[1] *Ex.*, 21, 17.   [2] *Mt.*, 15, 13.

And who would wish to join with these men who do not even admit
their own acts? For those who in their own councils, some ten or
more as we said above, wrote divers things, are clearly accusing
themselves in each one. The same is happening to them as then
⁵ happened to the traitors the Jews. For just as the latter, when
they left the one source of living water, dug for themselves wells
unable to hold water[1] — for so it is written in Jeremiah the prophet
— likewise the former, opposing the ecumenical council, have dug
for themselves many councils, and all useless for them since they
¹⁰ are seen to be like a sheaf with no strength. So let us not admit those
who name * the council of Ariminum or any other save that held   * p. 19
at Nicaea. For even those who quote the council of Ariminum seem
not to know what took place there. For have not even you, beloved,
learned from those among you who went to Ariminum how Ursacius
¹⁵ and Valens and Eudoxus and Auxentius — and there was there
with them also Demophilus — were deposed for wishing to write
things other than the decrees of Nicaea? And when they were
required to anathematise the Arian heresy, they refused and wished
rather to become supporters of the same. But the bishops, true
²⁰ servants and lovers of the Lord and orthodox believers, who were
about two hundred, wrote that Nicaea sufficed alone, and that
people were not to enquire or reflect any more or less than that.
These decisions they made known to Constantine who had ordered the
council to take place. But those who had been deposed at Ariminum,
²⁵ when they went to Constantine, he caused to be dishonoured,
and he had threats made against those who showed themselves
opposed to these decisions, that they should not return to their
dioceses but suffer restraint in Thrace that winter, so that they
would not acknowledge their innovations.
³⁰   **4** So if some quote the (council) of Ariminum, let them first
show the deposition of those who were mentioned above, and what
the bishops wrote when they said that they sought nothing more
than was confessed by the Fathers in Nicaea, and that people should
name no other council except that one. But they conceal this and
³⁵ instead proffer the acts forcibly carried through in Thrace, whereby

[1] Cf. *Jer.*, 2, *13.*

they are shown to be of the Arian heresy and opponents of the right faith. And if one wished to investigate closely the great council and those of theirs, he would find after the piety of the former the irrationality of the latter. Those who gathered in Nicaea * did not   *p. 20
5 come together after their deposition, but confessed that the holy Spirit is of the substance of the Father and the Son. But these, even after being deposed once, twice and three times at Ariminum, dared to write that one cannot say that God has either substance or hypostasis. And from this we can see, brethren, that those in
10 Nicaea lacked [1] the expressions of the Scriptures, God Himself saying in Exodus : « I am He who is [2] », and through Jeremiah : « Who stood in his hypostasis and saw his word ? [3] » and a little later : « if they stood in my hypostasis, and if they heard my words [4] ». And if hypostasis is substance, it has no other meaning than « what
15 is », which Jeremiah calls « existence », saying : « They did not hear the voice of my existence [5] ». for hypostasis and substance are existence, since He is and is existence. Paul understood this when he wrote to the Hebrews : « Who is the radiance of glory, the image of his hypostasis [6] ».
20   But these who think they know the Scriptures and call them-selves wise, not wishing to impute hypostasis to God — for this they wrote at Ariminum and in their other councils — how were they not justly deposed for saying, they also like the fool in his heart : « There is no God [7] » ? But again the Fathers taught at Nicaea
25 that God the Word is not created or made, because they had read that : « Everything was made by Him [8] », and : « By Him everything was created and established [9] ». But these men, who are rather Arians than Christians, even in their other councils dared to say that He was created and one of the creatures of which the Word Him-
30 self is fashioner and maker. For if through Him everything was made and He is a creature, then He would also have created Him-self. And how can the created create, or how could He who created be created ?
  * 5   But they are not even thus ashamed at saying things for   *p. 21
35 which they are hated by all men, naively quoting the (council) of Ariminum although they were clearly deposed at it. And as for

---

[1] Sic !   [2] *Ex., 3, 14.*   [3] *Jer., 23, 18.*   [4] *Jer., 23, 22.*   [5] *Jer., 9, 9.*
[6] *Heb., 1, 3.*   [7] *Ps., 13, 1.*   [8] *Jn., 1, 3.*   [9] *Coloss., 1, 16.*

the expression « the Son is consubstantial with the Father » which was written down aʋ Nicaea, and because of which they are accustomed to oppose the council and buzz like gnats everywhere because of this expression — either in their ignorance they stumble at it,
5 like those who stumble at the stone which was placed as a stumbling block in Zion [1], or they are aware, but because of it they oppose it and continually murmur, as it is truly an accurate sentence against their heresy. For it is not the words which pain them, but the condemnation they have in them. Furthermore they are the cause
10 of these themselves : even if knowingly they wish to hide them, yet it is fitting for us to speak, that by them the correspondence with the truth of the great council may be shown.

For the assembled bishops wished to reject the words of impiety invented by the Arians, namely : « from what is not », and calling the
15 Son « created and made », and : « there was a time when He was not », and : « He is of mutable nature », but to write what is confessed by the Scriptures, that : « He is from God by nature the only-begotten Son, who is the Word, the power and sole wisdom of the Father, true God [2] », as John said, and : « the radiance of glory and image of the
20 hypostasis of the Father [3] », as Paul wrote. But the Eusebians, seduced by vainglory, said : « Let us agree with each other, since we also are from God. For God is one from whom is everything [4] », and : « The old things have passed, behold they have been made new. But everything is of God [5] ». And they also thought what is
25 written in the Shepherd : « Before everything believe that God is one, who created and established all things and brought them into being from non-existence [6] ».

* But when the bishops saw their wicked cunning and the evil   * p. 22
machinations of their impiety, they declared the more clearly the
30 phrase « from God », and wrote that : « The Son is from the substance of the Father », in order that created things might be said not to exist by themselves without a cause, but to have their principle of existence from God, and the Son alone to be peculiar to the substance of the Father. For that is the characteristic of the only-
35 begotten and true Word of the Father; and this is the cause of writing « consubstantial ». And again when the bishops asked them,

[1] Cf. *Is.*, 8, *14*, 28, *16*; *Rom.*, 9, *33*.   [2] *Jn.*, 1, *14*; I *Cor.*, 1, *24*.   [3] *Heb.*, 1, *3*.
[4] I *Cor.*, 8, *6*.   [5] II *Cor.*, 5, *17-18*.   [6] Hermas *Mand.*, 1.

who seemed to be few, whether they said the Son was not created
but the power and sole wisdom of the Father, and the eternal image
of the Father immutable in everything and true God, the Eusebians were caught agreeing with each other that this happens also
5 to us. For we also are called the image and glory of God; and it
is said of us : « For we are they who live for ever[1]». We are the
many hosts : « And all the hosts of God went out from the land
of Egypt[2] »; The caterpillar and locust are called « a great host[3] »;
and « the Lord of hosts is with us, and the God of Jacob is our pro-
10 tector[4] ». And we have not merely the fact of being his, but He
calls us brothers. If we call the Son also true God it does not worry
us, since He is so truly.

6 This is the perverted thought of the Arians. But the bishops,
seeing thereby the fraud, collected from the Scriptures the (ex-
15 pressions) : « radiance[5] », «source[6]», « light[7] » and «image of the
hypostasis[8]», and : « by your light we see light[9] », and : « I and
my Father are one[10] ». And then very clearly and succinctly they
wrote that the Son is consubstantial with the Father. For all that
has been said above has this meaning. And their murmuring that
20 these expressions are not in the Scriptures * is refuted by themselves   * p. 23
to be vain, for their impieties are not drawn from the Scriptures.
Unscriptural are : « from non-existence », and : « There was a time
when He was not ». They make excuses that they have been condemned for unscriptural words despite their pious thoughts, for
25 they spoke as if they derived truly[11] from a dung-heap and from
the earth. But the bishops did not find words themselves, but
having a witness for themselves from the Fathers, so wrote. The
previous bishops before them, about one hundred and thirty, in
great Rome and also from our own city, condemned those
30 who called the Son « made» and «not consubstantial with the Father».
And Eusebius, who was bishop of Caesarea, knew this, who
first concurred with the Arian heresy, but finally signed the council
of Nicaea; he wrote assuring his party : « We know some former
lettered and knowledgeable bishops and writers who used the
35 expression 'consubstantial' of the divinity of the Father and the Son».

---

[1] II *Cor.*, 4, 11.   [2] *Ex.*, 12, 41.   [3] Cf. *Joel 2, 25.*   [4] *Ps.*, 45, 8.   [5] *Heb.*, 1, 3.   [6] *Ps.*,
35, 10; *Joel 3, 18*; *Zech.*, 13, 1.   [7] *Is.*, 60, 1; *Jn.*, 1, 9. [8] *Heb.*, 1, 3. [9] *Ps.*, 35, 10. [10] *Jn.*,
10, 30.   [11] *Syr* : coldly (sic !).

7 Why then do they still quote the council of Ariminum at which they were deposed ? Why do they reject the council of Nicaea which their Fathers signed and at which they confessed that the Son is from the substance of and consubstantial with the Father ?
5 Why do they linger ? For they now oppose not only those who assembled at Nicaea but also the great bishops before them, and even their own party. So whose heirs and successors are they ? How can they call « Fathers » those whose confession they do not accept, which was composed in a proper and apostolic manner ?
10 And if they suppose they can speak in opposition, let them speak — or rather let them reply, in order to be refuted after falling upon themselves, * if they [1] believe the Son who said : « I and my Father * p. 24 are one [2] », and : « He who has seen me has seen the Father [3] ». « Yes, they say, we believe because they are scriptural». But if they
15 are asked to say how They are one, or how he who has seen the Son has seen the Father, they inevitably say « by similarity », unless they have completely abandoned the thoughts of their brothers who are called «Anomoeans». And if they are asked again in what way « similar », they say in their daring : « With perfect virtue
20 and harmony He wills the same as the Father, and does not will what the Father does not will ». But let them learn that to resemble the Father in virtue and will involves being mutable in will. But the Word is not thus, unless He is partly similar according to your argument but not similar in substance. But these are characteristics
25 of us creatures who have a created nature. For we also, even if we cannot be similar to God in substance, yet increasing in virtue we imitate God, the Lord having given us (this grace) saying : « Be merciful as your Father is merciful [4] », and : « Be perfect as your Father is perfect [5] ».
30   No one would deny that creatures are mutable : the angels transgressed and Adam disobeyed, and we all lack the grace of the Word. And what is mutable does not resemble the immutable, nor the created the creator. So we it was whom the saint was considering when he said : « O God, who will be similar to you [6] » ? and : « Who
35 is like you among the gods, O Lord [7] » ? He called gods those who were created but had partaken of the Word, as he said : « If they

---

[1] *Syr* : we.   [2] *Jn.*, 10, 30.   [3] *Jn.*, 14, 9.   [4] *Lk.*, 6, 36.   [5] *Mt.*, 5, 48.
[6] *Ps.*, 82, 2.   [7] *Ps.*, 85, 8; *Ex.*, 15, 11.

are gods among whom was the Word of God [1] ». And the things
which are shared are not always the same, nor similar to him by
whom they are shared. * So He said of Himself : « I and my Father   * p. 25
are one [2] », although created things are not like this. But let those
5 who in Ariminum chose this reply (whether) a created substance
could say : « What I see the Father doing, that I also do [3] ». For
creatures are made and not actors; and if not they would have
later made themselves. As they say : « The Son is created and the
Father made Him », the Son would certainly have made Himself,
10 since He is able to do what the Father does, as He said. But such
a thing is absurd and quite invalid, for nothing can make itself.

8 And again let them say if creatures are able to say : « All
that the Father has is mine [4] ». He has the faculty of creating and
establishing, of being eternal and omnipotent and without change.
15 But creatures are not able to acquire the faculty of creating, for
they are created, or of being eternal, for they have a beginning to
their existence, or of omnipotence or immutability, for their nature
is mutable and they are under authority, just as the Scriptures
say. If these are characteristics of the Son, they are not so by reason
20 of his virtue but of his substance, as we said. So it is clear, as the
council said, that He is not from another substance but from the
Father, as those properties are also. For the characteristics of the
substance of the Father are also the characteristics of what is born
from Him; and how would one call that except « consubstantial » ?
25 For what one sees in the Father, that he sees in the Son, the Son
not by participation [5] but by substance. And this is the (meaning
of) : « I and my Father are one [6] », and : « Who has seen me has
seen the Father [7] ».

Furthermore this also is a good way to demonstrate ⌐their
30 folly [8] : if it follows from virtue to will, * and the Son according   * p. 26
to us is similar to the Father by habits of virtue, which are
characteristics of action, it is clear that you say God is composed
of action and substance. And who would believe you if you said
that, for God is not composite, who constructed everything to
35 come into being ? And He is not such as are the things made by
Him through the Word. Far from it ! For substance is simple,

[1] *Jn.,* 10, *35.*   [2] *Jn.,* 10, *30.*   [3] Cf. *Jn.,* 5, *19.*   [4] *Jn.,* 16, *15.*   [5] *Syr* : after
substance (sic !)   [6] *Jn.,* 10, *30.*   [7] *Jn.,* 14, *9.*   [8] *Syr* : to them (sic !).

in which there is no operation or alteration or shadow of change [1],
as said James. For He is not revealed by virtue since there is no
operation in God or in the Son, for it is clear that He is co-eternal
with his substance. This you would certainly admit if your under-
5 standing had not completely perished. For being eternal and of
the same substance as God and being naturally from Him, what
would that be for you except thereby that the begotten is consubstantial with the begetter? For this is the proof of the property of
the Son with regard to the Father. And he who does not say this,
10 does not think that the Son is by nature and in truth the Word.

9 This was the thought of the Fathers when they wrote that
the Son is consubstantial with the Father, and anathematised
those who say that the Son is from another hypostasis; they did
not invent words for themselves, but they also learned from their
15 Fathers, as we said above. Now as these things have been so proved,
Ariminum is superfluous, and it is also superfluous that they should
quote any other council concerning the faith, for that of Nicaea is
sufficient, which also agrees with the former bishops and which
their own Fathers signed, whom they should have revered that
20 they might no longer be called many things rather than Christians.
* But if even after all these things, after the witness of the former   *p. 27
bishops, after the signature of their Fathers, they pretend [2] to be
ignorant and are afraid of the expression « consubstantial », let them
say and let them think that He is more simply Son by nature and
25 Son in truth, and let them anathematise, as the council commanded,
those who say the Son of God is made or created or from what does
not exist, or there was a time when the Son of God was not, because
He is immutable and unchanging and not from another hypostasis.
And thus let them flee from the Arian heresy, and trusting that
30 they strictly anathematise those men, let them immediately confess
that the Son is of the substance of and consubstantial with the
Father. For it was on that account that the Fathers, when they
called the Son consubstantial, immediately added : « And those
who say (He is) created or made or from what does not exist, or
35 there was a time when He was not, the Catholic church ana-
thematizes », in order that thereby they might know that the term

---

[1] *James, 1, 17.*   [2] *Syr : boast.*

« consubstantial» means that. And the force of « consubstantial»
is recognised from the statement that the Son is not a creature or
made. Whoever says the Word is consubstantial does not think
He is a creature; and whoever anathematises what was said above,
5 at the same time considers the Son to be consubstantial with the
Father; and saying « consubstantial», he calls Him the true and
beloved Son of the Father; and saying « beloved», he understands
the sayings : « I and my Father are one [1]», and : « Who has seen
me has seen the Father [2]».

10 **10** So it would have been fitting for us to write such things in
many words, but since we were writing to our acquaintances we
therefore expressed ourselves briefly, praying that the bond of
peace would be preserved by everyone and that all of the Catholic
church would say the same and think the same. And not as teaching
15 but as reminding you we are (sending this) to you. We are not alone
* in writing but (are joined by) all in Egypt and the Libyas, about * p. 28
ninety bishops. For this is the thought of all, and we always sign
for each other if it happens that some are not present. So being
thus disposed, because we happened to be assembled, we wrote
20 also to beloved Damasus, bishop of great Rome, about Auxentius
who had assailed the church of Mediolanum, telling of the
(charges) against him : that he is not only a member of the Arian
heresy, but also guilty of many wicked acts which he performed
with Gregory his companion in impiety, and we were surprised that
25 up to now he had not been deposed and expelled from the church.
And let us thank his piety and that of those who assembled in
Rome, that expelling the party of Ursacius and Valentinus and
those who thought the same, they have preserved the unanimity
of the Catholic church, which we pray may be also kept by you,
30 as we said above, with those who proposed a rabble of councils
on the excuse of the faith — that in Ariminum, that in Sirmium,
that in Isauria, that in Thrace, those in Constantinople, those
frequently held in Antioch. But of all these let there prevail among
you only the faith which was confessed in Nicaea by the Fathers,
35 which was signed also by the Fathers of those who now oppose it,
as we said above, that the Apostle may say also on our account :

[1] *Jn.*, 10, *30*.   [2] *Jn.*, 14, *9*.

« I praise you because you have remembered all my commands,
and as the traditions which I handed down to you, so have you
kept them [1] ».

11 For this council of Nicaea is in truth the laying-bare of
[5] every impious heresy; it also refutes those who blaspheme against
the holy Spirit and say He is created. For when the Fathers spoke
concerning belief in the Son, they immediately added : * « We believe   * p. 29
also in the holy Spirit », in order that, confessing the faith in the
holy Trinity as perfect and complete, they might declare in it the
[10] image of the faith of Christ and the teaching of the Catholic church.
For it was clear to you and to all, and no Christian in this matter
gainsays to hold this opinion, that our faith is not in creation but
in one God, who is known in the holy and perfect Trinity, into
which being also baptised and in it united to the Godhead, we
[15] believe that we shall also inherit the kingdom of heaven in Jesus
Christ our Lord, through whom be praise and power to the Father
with the holy Spirit for ever and ever. Amen.

End of the Letter of the Holy and Blessed Athanasius.

[1] 1 *Cor.*, 11, 2.

1 Athanasius and the bishops who were present in Alexandria
to their fellow ministers in the Lord, greeting. We are convinced
that as you are servants of God and stewards you are able to settle
⁵ all the affairs of the church. But because it has reached us that,
although formerly many were cut off from us by contention, they
now wish to make peace, and many abandoning the alliance of the
Arians are anxious for communion with us, it was necessary for
us and our beloved Eusebius and Asterius to write these things to
¹⁰ your graces, who are truly beloved and fellow ministers and dear
to us, since you ¹ rejoice at such a report and pray that if any
one has been left far from us, and all who still seem in conjunction
with the Arians, may abandon communion with them, so that
henceforth all men everywhere may say : « One Lord, one faith ² ».
¹⁵ For « what is so fine, or what so sweet, as the Psalmist said, as for
brothers to live in unity ³ » ? For it is just that (our) house be the
church and (our) thoughts identical. For so we believe that the Lord
dwells with us, as He says : « I shall dwell among you and shall
walk with you ⁴ », and : « Here I shall dwell because I loved it ⁵ ».
²⁰ And where is « here » ? It is where piety and one faith are preached.

2 So we from Egypt also truly wished to come immediately
with our beloved Eusebius and Asterius for many reasons, but
especially for this, that we might at once embrace * your love and   * p. 31
together enjoy such peace and concord. But because ecclesiastical
²⁵ necessities keep us back, as we explained in those other letters
and as you can learn from our colleagues themselves, we were grieved,
but nevertheless thought it right that our fellow ministers Eusebius
and Asterius should come to you instead of us. And thanks to their
piety, although they were anxious to go to their dioceses ⁶, first
³⁰ of all they made their way to you on account of the pressing need
of the church. And when they agreed, we were consoled that as
they and you meet there, we all may be thought to be with you.

---

¹ Sic ! ² *Eph.*, 4, 5. ³ *Ps.*, 132, 1. ⁴ IICor., 6, 16; cf. *Lev.*, 26, 12. ⁵ *Ps.*, 131, 14.
⁶ *Syr* : diocese.

3 So all those who wish to make peace with us, and especially those now assembled in the Old (church) and those who have abandoned the Arians, call to yourselves, and as fathers their sons take them to yourselves, and receive them as teachers and guardians. [5] When you have joined them to your loved ones, those with Paulinus[1], ask no more from them than that they anathematize the Arian heresy and confess the faith which was confessed by the Fathers in Nicaea, and that they anathematize those who say that the holy Spirit is created and separate from the substance of the [10] Son. For this is truly to abandon the foul heresy of the Arians, not to divide the Trinity or say that any part thereof is created. For those who pretend to quote the faith confessed at Nicaea but dare to blaspheme against the holy Spirit, do nothing more than deny the Arian heresy with words, but hold it in their minds. So [15] let the impiety of Sabellius and of Paul of Samosata and of Valentinus and of Basilides, and the madness of the Manichaeans be anathematized by all. And when this is so done, after all evil opinions have been abolished by everyone, only the faith of the Catholic church will be shown to be pure.

[20] * **4** That such is the faith held by us and by those who have * p. 32 continually kept our communion, we think that neither you nor any one else ignores, but because we rejoice with those who wish to reunite[2] with all, and especially with those assembled in the Old (church), we now praise[3] God for all of them and also for this good [25] intention of theirs. We urge you that by these conditions their accord may be won, and that nothing more than these be asked by us[4], as we said above, and that those assembled in the Old (church) and those with Paulinus propose nothing other and nothing more than was written at Nicaea.

[30] **5** So the letter which was spread abroad by everyone as if it had been composed at the synod of Sardica concerning the faith, prevent it from circulating or being read, since the synod defined nothing like that. For some men have taken it upon themselves to write about the faith of the synod of Nicaea as if it were insufficient, [35] and they have daringly attempted (to complete it). But the holy synod which met at Sardica defined that nothing more should be

---

[1] *Syr* : Flavianus.   [2] *Syr* : to be ashamed (sic !).   [3] *Syr* : are found (sic !).   [4] Sic !

written about the faith, but that the faith confessed by the Fathers
at Nicaea suffices, because it lacks nothing and is full of piety;
and that it is not right to set out the faith a second time, lest that
written at Nicaea seem not to be complete, and an excuse be provided
5 for those who seek to write and define the faith many times. Con-
sequently, if any one propose this or something else, silence such
people and rather make them keep the peace, for there seems to
us to be nothing in them save contention only. For those whom
some blame as saying three hypostases, because the expressions
10 are not scriptural and are therefore suspicious, we consider to seek [1]
nothing further * than the confession of Nicaea. However, we excom-   * p. 33
municate them for their contentiousness, lest like the Arians they
say (the hypostases) are separate and foreign and different in
substance from each other, and that each hypostasis is distinct
15 by itself as are the other creatures and those born from men; or
like separate substances, or as are gold and silver and brass they
call them such; or as other heretics call them three principles and
three gods, they think likewise and say three hypostases. They
averred that they neither say nor had ever thought thus. But when
20 we asked them : « Then how do you say these things, or why do
you use these words ? » they replied : « Because we believe in the
holy Trinity, we know the Trinity not in name only but in truth
to exist and subsist, since the Father truly exists and subsists,
and the Son truly exists and subsists, and the holy Spirit truly
25 subsists and exists ». They did not say three Gods or three principles,
nor did they at all endure those who said or thought so, but : « We
know the holy Trinity, one Godhead and one principle; and the
Son consubstantial with the Father, as the Fathers said; and the
holy Spirit not created or foreign, but of the same substance as
30 the Son and inseparable ».

6 So (accepting) their explanation of these expressions and
excuse, we examined [2] also those who were blamed by them for
saying one hypostasis, whether they were thinking like Sabellius
and likewise speaking for the suppression of the Son and the holy
35 Spirit, as if the Son was without substance and the holy Spirit
without hypostasis. They also averred that they had never said

---

[1] *Syr* : that we seek (sic !).   [2] *Syr* : but (sic !).

* or thought so : « But we say hypostasis, considering that it is the * p. 34
same to say hypostasis and substance. And we think He is one,
because the Son is of the substance of the Father, and because of
the identity of nature. For the Godhead is one and we believe that
[5] his nature is one, and not that that of the Father is different and
that the Son and the holy Spirit are foreign to it ». Thus those who
had been blamed for saying three hypostases also agreed with them.
And those who said one substance, when their expressions were
explained admitted them also. So both parties anathematized
[10] Arius as contending with Christ, and Sabellius and Paul of Samosata
as impious, and Valentinus and Basilides as strangers to the truth,
and Mani as an inventor of evil. And they all by the grace of God
with such explanations nevertheless [1] agreed that better and more
accurate than such expressions was the faith confessed in Nicaea
[15] by the Fathers, and that the rest of the expressions of that synod
would rather suffice for them.

7 But since some men saw good to quarrel among themselves
also over the dispensation of our Saviour in the flesh, we examined [2]
both the latter and the former. And the former agreed with what
[20] the latter confessed, that not as the Word of the Lord was in the
prophets did He also likewise dwell in a holy man at the end of the
ages, but the Word became flesh; and although He was in the form
of God, He took the form of a servant and was born of Mary in the
flesh a man for our sake; and in this way the race of men, being
[25] completely and fully liberated from sin and saved from the dead,
enters the kingdom of heaven. And they confessed this also, that
the Saviour did not have a body without a soul or without sense
or without a mind, for it was not possible that when * the Lord became * p. 35
man for our sake his body should be without a mind. Salvation not
[30] of the body only but also of the soul was effected in the Word.
And although He is truly the Son of God, He also became a man [3];
and although He was the only-begotten Son of God, the same
became the first-born among many brethren [4]. Therefore neither
was one the Son of God who was before Abraham and another
[35] who was after Abraham, nor was one He who raised Lazarus and
another who enquired after him, but it was the same one who said

---

[1] Sic! [2] *Syr* : but (sic!). [3] *Syr* : son of man. [4] Cf., *Rom.*, 8. 29.

in human fashion : « Where lies Lazarus [1] ? » and in divine fashion
raised him up. It was the same one who spat in human fashion
like a man, and in divine fashion as the Son of God opened the
eyes of the man blind from birth. And He suffered in the flesh,
5 as Peter said [2], but in divine fashion opened the tombs and raised
the dead. From which, understanding in this way everything in
the gospel, they averred that they entertained identical opinions
concerning the incarnation and becoming man of God.

8 So since they have made this confession, we urge you not
10 to condemn or reject hastily those who make such a confession and
so explain the words they utter, but rather receive them among you
since they have explained and apologised. But those who do not
wish to make such a confession or explain their words, those restrain
and forsake as having suspicious opinions. And (not) following
15 them, advise those who explain and think correctly not to judge
each other further, nor to contend with words on a subject without
profit, nor to quarrel with such expressions, but to agree on the
expression of piety. For those who do not think thus but merely
argue with such slogans * and seek beyond what was written at   * p. 36
20 Nicaea, do nothing other than give as drink to their neighbours
dregs of destruction [3], being jealous of peace and loving divisions.
But do you, like good men and faithful servants and stewards of
the Lord, make silent and prevent the things which cause scandal
and are innovations, and more than anything else first choose such
25 peace without compromising the faith, that perchance the Lord
will have pity on us and will gather together those now sundered,
and we shall all be one flock and have one head, our Lord Jesus Christ.

9 So since it is not right for us to seek anything more than
the synod of Nicaea or to admit the expressions of contention [4],
30 for the sake of the peace for which we have been solicitous by
seeking not to expel those who hold the correct faith, what they
confessed we have briefly set down, we who were left in Alexandria,
together with our colleagues Eusebius and Asterius, for many of
us had set out for their dioceses. But do you, when you are as-
35 sembled as you are accustomed and have summoned every one
there to you, read this out, for it is right that first the letter should

---

[1] *Jn.*, 11, *34.*   [2] I *Pet.*, 4, 1.   [3] Cf. *Hab.*, 2, *15*; *Ps*, 74, 9.   [4] *Syr* : joy (sic !).

be read there. And there unite those who are anxious and zealous for peace. And then when they are united, where it seems good to all the people, there conclude the assembly, and in common all praise the Lord.

5   Greet all the brethren who are with you. The brethren with us greet you.

End of the Encyclical Letter of Saint Athanasius.

1 On reading what you wrote to us I praised your virtue, but
at the impudence of those who understand nothing of what they
⁵ say and are ignorant about what they are contending I was greatly
amazed, and I endeavoured to be truly silent. For if one would
reply concerning things which are so obvious and clearer than the
sun, it would seem nothing other than an excuse for presumption
for those who are so impious. And this we have learned from Christ
¹⁰ our Saviour : when Pilate washed his hands because he realised
the hatred and calumny of the Jews, He made no reply, but to
Pilate's wife He showed a vision, only in order that not by words
but by deeds and power our Lord might be believed to be God
above all when He was hanging on the cross ; and again by not
¹⁵ replying to the harassing of Caiaphas, by his silence He turned all
men to Himself.

So although I payed no attention because I had seen the contentiousness and impudence of these disputators, I was at length put to
shame by your zeal on behalf of the truth ; and I have put nothing
²⁰ in writing save what was written by you, that by what our opponents
reject they may now be persuaded to keep their tongues from
speaking evil and their lips from uttering deceit. And would that
they did not revile ¹ Him who hung on the cross, with the Jews
who earlier said : « If He is the Son of God, * let Him come down   * p. 38
²⁵ from the cross ² ». But if they will not be silent, do you remember
the word of the Apostle who says : « A heretic after one correction
and a second reject, knowing that he is perverse and sins and
brings condemnation on himself ³ ». For if they are Gentiles or
Jews who dare to tell such tales, like the Jews let them consider
³⁰ the cross of Christ a stumbling block, or like the Gentiles as
foolishness. But if they pretend to be like Christians, let them learn
that Christ who was crucified is the Lord of glory and the power
and wisdom of God.

---

¹ *Syr* : lack (sic !).   ² *Mt.*, 27, *40*; *Mk.*, 15, *30*.   ³ *Titus* 3, *10-11.*

2 But if they doubt whether He is the true God, let them revere Thomas who touched Him who was crucified and declared Him his Lord and his God. Let them also fear the Lord Himself, who after He had washed the feet of his disciples, said to them : 5 « You call me 'our master and our lord' and you do well, for I am [1] ». For in the body in which He was when He washed his disciples' feet, in the same He took up our sins onto the cross. And there was testimony concerning Him that He is Lord of creation when the sun held back its rays, and the earth shook, and the rocks 10 were split, and the veil was rent, and the dead who were asleep arose, and the centurion recognised that Christ who had been crucified was truly the Son of God. For it was no other man's, the visible body, but God's, who in it had been crucified and had given life to the dead.

15 Nor is their other audacity befitting when they say that the Word of God was in a holy man — for indeed He was in the prophets and the other saints — as He would then be found to be born each time and die many times. But it was not so. Far from it ! But once at the end of ages for the elimination of sin the Word became body 20 from the Virgin Mary, and was born a complete man in our form for our sake, as * the holy scriptures say and as He Himself said : * p. 39 « Why do you seek to kill me, who spoke words of truth with you [2] ? » And the Jews said to Him : « Not because of them do we kill you ; for you are a man and you make yourself God [3] ». We do not partake 25 of the body of a man, but we partake of the body of God the Word who died on our behalf the death of the cross.

3 I was also amazed at this other thing, how they dared to suppose that He became man in the order of nature. For if this were so, Mary and her remembrance would be superfluous, for 30 nature does not know of a virgin able to give birth without a man. Therefore by the will of the Father, God the Word became man bodily for our salvation, in order to have what He might offer on our behalf and to give life to all of us, to those who by the fear of death were all the time in servitude. For no man gave himself to 35 death for our sake, because all men are condemned to death through the saying : « Dust you are and to dust will you return [4] » ; and it

---

[1] *Jn.*, 13, *13.*   [2] *Jn.*, 8, *40.*   [3] *Jn.*, 10, *33.*   [4] *Gen.*, 3, *19.*

applies to all men. And again David said : « What man is there
who will live and not see death, and will deliver himself from the
hand of Sheol [1] » ? And nothing of creation suffered on our behalf,
but God the Word offered his own body for us, that our faith and
5 our hope might not be in a man but in God, and that we might
have faith in God the Word. And furthermore, when He became
man « we saw, as is written, his glory as the glory of God, full of
grace and truth [2] ». For what Christ accepted willingly, He mag-
nified as God. He was hungry bodily, and satisfied the hungry
10 divinely. And if any one is offended at these bodily things, let
him believe in what He did as God. He asked about Lazarus as a
man, but raised him up with power as God. When some one says
suckling or infant or swaddling clothes or lying * in a manger, or * p. 40
growing up or eating or drinking or death, let him not be offended,
15 lest being offended at those things which were done for our salvation,
he be offended also at his advent for our sake. For as it was not by
the order of nature that He became man, so also when He did become
man it was fitting that He should show all those (attributes) which
are of men, lest the illusion of Mani and Marcion should prevail
20 with that of the other heretics who are godless. It was fitting again
that when He became body He should make known through his
works that He was truly God, lest Paul of Samosata find a pretext,
who said that He was a different man other than God the Word.

4 So (let) the unbeliever understand the following : He was an
25 infant in the manger and forced the Magi to come and worship
Him ; when He was young He went down to Egypt and overthrew the
idols of Egypt ; when He ascended the cross He raised up those who
had been buried for a long time ; the same is God who became man
for our sake. And it is clear to all that not for his own sake but
30 for theirs He endured everything, that we by his sufferings might
put on impassibility and incorruptibility and obtain everlasting life.

5 These things I have written to you based on your own letter,
as I said above, adding or subtracting nothing but speaking only
of the cross, in order that what was a stumbling block to the weak
35 might strengthen them to worship Christ crucified, who is the
true God, in whom we are baptised by his saving passion. But do

[1] Ps., 88, 49. [2] Jn., 1, 14.

you lovingly persuade the unbelievers, who are the new Jews, that He who was born, the same is God above all, and He endured the passion and performed miracles. And perhaps they will progress from ignorance to the knowledge of the truth, and believe that
5 He who was born of Mary, the same is God from God, who was in the beginning with God, by whom all things were made, and He willingly accepted the birth of men and endured everything that follows birth, as far as death, the death of the cross, as we said above. If these remarks do not suffice for what you wrote, it would
10 be good for us to add * against their craftiness this also, that they *p. 41 should not be ashamed of anything they dared (to say) as if convicted, but as if we had reminded them that they stray not from the truth. For the faith of our Fathers who (assembled) in the city of Nicaea is true and suffices for the overthrow of all impious heresies, especially
15 that of the Arians who blaspheme against God the Word, and perforce also speak impiously against the holy Spirit.

Greet all those who believe aright. All the brethren who are with us greet you, remembering your virtue.

The end of the Letter to Maximus the Philosopher.

1 To the dear and beloved Adelphus, bishop and confessor, Athanasius and the brethren, greeting in the Lord. Having read what was written by your holiness we truly approved of your piety
5 in Christ; and we especially praised God for giving you such grace that you might hold the correct belief to realise as far as possible the wiles of the devil. But we were amazed at the infamy of the heretics in seeing to what a depth of impiety they have sunk, so that they no longer preserve their senses but on all sides have a
10 perverted mind. The instigation of this hateful thing is from the devil and the imitation of the lawless Jews. For just as the latter when [2] refuted on every side found for themselves excuses [3] merely to deny the Lord and bring against themselves the prophecies, in the same way the former, when they see that they are everywhere [4]
15 notorious and that their heresy is abhorred by all men [5], become inventors of evil, ⌐so that not desisting [6] from fighting the truth they continue [7] truly combating with Christ. For whence sprang up for them this evil shoot? How did they even dare to utter this new blasphemy against the Saviour? But as is likely, the impious
20 one is truly evil * and reprobate in the faith. For first denying the   * p. 43 divinity of the Only-begotten Son of God they pretended to admit at least his coming in the flesh; but now, sinking lower they have fallen away even from this opinion of theirs, so that they have become atheists in every way, with the result that they neither
25 recognise God nor believe that He became man. For if they had believed they would not have uttered such things as your holiness wrote against them.

2 You therefore dear one and truly beloved by all, have done what befits the ecclesiastical tradition and piety in the Lord by
30 refuting and admonishing and rebuking such people; because being ⌐animated by [8] their father the devil they neither knew nor understood, as it is written, but were walking in darkness [9]. Let them

---

[1] The Letter of the same saint Athanasius A.   [2] when *om.* B.   [3] an excuse B.
[4] + when they see that openly A (sic!).   [5] men *om.* B.   [6] lest, desisting B.   [7] they are A.   [8] entangled with B.   [9] *Ps.*, 81, 5.

learn from your honour that such evil notions as theirs belong to
Valentinus, Marcion and the Manichaeans. Some of them exchanged
the truth for supposition; others, dividing the indivisible, denied
that « the Word became flesh and dwelt among us [1] ». Why therefore
[5] when they entertain these men's opinions do they not become as [2]
heirs also to their names ? For it is suitable that when they share
their evil opinion they should also take their names [3], to be called
henceforth Valentinians and Marcionites and Manichaeans, so
that perhaps being ashamed at the foulness [4] of the names they
[10] may thereby be able [5] to realise to what a depth of impiety they
have sunk. And it would be right to make no more reply to these
men, according to the advice * of the Apostle which runs : « A man   * p. 44
that is a heretic after one admonition and a second reject, knowing
that such a man is perverted and sins, being condemned by himself[6] ».
[15] And the prophet also particularly speaks of such people : « The
foolish man will speak foolish things, and his heart will consider
vanities [7] ». But since like their head they also go about like lions
seeking which of the simple they may devour, therefore we had
to reply in writing to your honour, that the brethren being instructed
[20] by your understanding may all the more reprove the vanity of
their words.

   3   We do not worship creation. Far from it ! For such is the
error of the heathen and the Arians. But we worship the Lord of
creation [8] who was incarnate, the Word of God. For even if the
[25] flesh by itself is a part of creation, yet it became the body of God.
And not this body itself, separating it from the Word, do we worship,
nor wishing to worship the Word do we divide Him from his flesh ;
but knowing, as we said above, that the Word became flesh, Him
we recognise as God also incarnate in the flesh [9]. Who then is so
[30] foolish as to say to the Lord : « Stand aside from the body that I
may worship you » ? Or who is so impious as to say to Him with
the senseless [10] Jews because of the body : « Why do you, being a
man, make yourself God [11] » ?

---

[1] *Jn.*, 1, *14.*   [2] as *om.* B.   [3] name B.   [4] vanity A.   [5] + also A.   [6] *Titus*
3, *10-11.*   [7] *Is.*, 32, *6.*   [8] of creatures A.   [9] Cf., *Jn.*, 1, *14.*   [10] sense
om. B.   [11] Cf. *Jn.*, 10, *33.*

But not such was the leper, for he worshipped * God incarnate * p. 45
in the body and knew that He was God, saying : « Lord, if you
wish you can heal me [1] ». He neither supposed the Word of God
to be a creature on account of the flesh, nor despised the flesh
[5] which He had put on because of the fact that the Word is the
maker of all creation, ⌐but he worshipped the Creator of all as
<in> the created temple and was cleansed [2]. So also the woman with
an issue of blood, believing and merely touching the hem of his
cloak, was healed; and the sea that was foaming with waves heard
[10] the incarnate Word and ceased from the storm; for the man blind
from his mother's womb was healed by the Word with the spittle
of the flesh. And what is greater and more amazing — for [3] perhaps
this caused even the most impious to stumble — even when the
Lord was hanging on the cross, for his was the body and the Word
[15] was in it, the sun was darkened, the earth shook, the rocks were
rent, the veil of the temple was split, and many bodies ⌐of those
who [4] had formerly fallen asleep arose.

4 This took place without anyone considering whether it was
right to believe in the incarnate Word, as now the Arians presume
[20] to do. But though seeing Him a man they knew Him to be their
creator, and hearing a human voice they did not say because of
the humanity that the Word was a creature, but rather trembled
and realised nothing less than that He was speaking from his holy
temple. How then are these impious ones not afraid lest, since
[25] they did not judge that they had God in their ken, they may be
given over to a reprobate mind to do those things which are not
right [5] ? For creation does not worship a creature, nor again on
account of the flesh does she refuse * to worship her Lord, but she * p. 46
saw her Maker in a body; « And at the name of Jesus Christ every
[30] knee bowed, and bows, of things in heaven and things on earth
and things under the earth, and every tongue confesses that Jesus
Christ is Lord to the glory of God the Father [6] », even if it does
not please the Arians.

For the body did not bring dishonour to the Word. Far from it !
[35] But rather He is honoured by it. Nor because the Son who is in
the form of the Father took the form of a servant was He diminished

---

[1] *Mt.*, 8, 2; *Mk.*, 1, 40; *Lk.*, 5, 12.   [2] but … cleansed *om.* A.   [3] for *om.* B.   [4] which
B.   [5] Cf. *Rom.*, 1, 28.   [6] *Philipp.*, 2, 10-11.

in divinity, but rather He was the liberator of all [1] flesh and of all
creation. And even if God sent his Son and He was born of a woman,
the matter does not bring shame upon us but rather good repute
and great blessing. For He became a man to make us divine in
[5] Him, and He came from a woman and was born of a virgin to transfer
to Himself our birth which was in error, and that we might henceforth
become a holy race and sharers in the divine nature [2], just as the
blessed Peter wrote. « And what was impossible for the law in as
much as it was weak because of the flesh, God by sending his Son
[10] in the form of flesh of sin, and because of sin, condemned sin in
the flesh [3] ».

   5   The flesh then which was taken by the Word that He might
free all men and raise them all up from the dead and deliver them
all from sin — how then do those who despise it, who because of
[15] it denounce the Son of God as fashioned and [4] a creature, not
appear ungrateful and worthy of all hatred ? For [5] they not only
cry to God, saying : « Do not send your only-begotten Son in the
flesh ; do not make Him take a body from a virgin, lest He save
us from death and sin. We do not wish Him to be born in the body
[20] lest He accept death on our behalf ; * we do not want the Word to   * p. 47
become flesh, lest in Him we have a mediator for the path towards
You and we inhabit the mansions of heaven. Let the gates of heaven
be shut, lest through the veil [6] of his flesh your Word renew for us
the path to [7] heaven ».
[25]   These then are their cries which are uttered with devilish
effrontery in that they have found for themselves ⌐a wicked in-
vention [8]. For those who do not wish to worship the Word made
flesh deny his becoming man, and those who divide the Word from
the flesh think there was neither one salvation from sin nor loosing
[30] from death. And where [9] do these impious ones indeed find the
flesh by itself which our Saviour accepted so that they dare to
say : « We do not worship the Lord with the flesh, but we separate
the body and Him only we serve » ? So the blessed Stephen even
in heaven saw the Lord standing on the right hand, and the angels
[35] said to the disciples : « Thus He will come as you saw Him going
to heaven [10] ». And the Lord Himself said, crying to the Father :

---

[1] of his own A.   [2] Cf. II *Pet.*, 1, *4*.   [3] *Rom.*, 8, *3*.   [4] of B.   [5] but B.   [6] gateway A.
[7] of A.   [8] absurd wickedness B.   [9] how A.   [10] *Acts*, 1, *11*.

« I wish that where I am they also may be with me at all times [1] ».
And indeed if [2] the flesh is indivisible from the Word, must they
not put aside their error and worship henceforth the Father [3] in
the name of Jesus Christ our Lord, or if they do not worship and
5 serve the Word who became flesh, be cast out on every side and
no longer be numbered among the Christians, but either with the
heathen or the present Jews?

* **6** Such then is the madness and daring of these men, as we * p. 48
said above. But our faith is orthodox ˹which stems from the apostolic
10 teaching [4] and the tradition of the Fathers; it is confirmed by the
New and Old Testaments and by the prophets who say : « Send
your Word and your truth [5] »; and : « Behold a virgin will conceive
and bear a son, and they will call his name Emmanuel, which is
when interpreted : 'our God is with us [6]' ». And what is this save
15 that God will be born in the flesh? And the apostolic tradition
teaches, blessed Peter speaking : « Christ therefore suffered for us
in the flesh [7] ». And Paul writes : « As we expect the blessed hope
and revelation of the glory of the great [8] God and our Saviour
Jesus Christ, who gave Himself for us to save us from all impiety
20 and purify for Himself an abundant people zealous for good works [9] ».
How then would He have given Himself for us unless He had put
on flesh? For when He offered this He gave Himself for us, in order
that when He partook of death in it He might destroy the devil
who holds the power of death. Therefore we at all times confess
25 the name of Jesus Christ, and we do not reject the grace which
came to us through Him. For his coming in the flesh was salvation
from death and the deliverance of all creation.

So dear one and beloved of all, let those who love the Lord
reflect on these things; but those who imitate the way of Judas
30 and have abandoned the Lord to be with Caiaphas, let them be
instructed by them, whether they will or whether they be ashamed.
And let them know that when we worship the Lord in the flesh
we do not serve a creature [10] but the Creator who put on a created [11]
body, as I said above.

---

1 *Jn., 17, 24.* 2 if *om.* B. 3 the Father *om.* A. 4 which ... teaching *om.* A.
5 *Ps., 42, 3.* 6 *Is., 7, 14; Mt., 1, 23.* 7 *I Pet., 4, 1.* 8 great *om.* B. 9 *Titus 2,*
13-14. 10 creation A. 11 visible A.

* p. 49

7 We wish your honour to ask them this. When the sons of
Israel were commanded to go up to Jerusalem to worship in the
temple of the Lord, where is the ark and above it the cherubim
of glory who overshadow the mercy-seat, did they do well or the
⁵ opposite? If then they acted wickedly, how by neglecting this law
would they have fallen under punishment? For it is written :
« Everyone who scorns ¹ and does not go up will be destroyed from
his people ² ». But ³ if they did well and were thereby pleasing to
God, how are the wicked Arians, more disgraceful than all heresies,
¹⁰ not worthy of destruction many times over, because they approve
of the ancient people for their reverence towards the temple, yet
do not wish to worship the Lord who is in the flesh as in a temple?
Although the temple of that time was fashioned from stones and
gold, like a shadow, yet when the truth came the type no longer
¹⁵ continued, and there remained in it no stone upon a stone which
was not overthrown, according to the saying of the Lord ⁴. And
when they saw the temple of stones they did not think that the
Lord who spoke in the temple was also a creature, ⌐nor when they
went to a distance and worshipped did they despise the temple ⁵,
²⁰ but they entered it ⁶ lawfully and served God, making use of the
temple.

Since this was the case, how is the body of the Lord not truly
all-holy, which ⁷ was announced by the archangel Gabriel and
fashioned by the holy Spirit, and (which) became the garment of
²⁵ the Word and a temple and inseparable instrument? So it was a
bodily hand which the Word stretched out to raise the woman
with a fever; and He uttered a voice when He raised * Lazarus from
the dead; and again, when ⌐He stretched out his hands ⁸ on the
cross He overthrew the prince of the dominion of the air who now
³⁰ operates in the sons of disobedience, and purified our way to heaven.

* p. 50

8 So he who despises the temple despises the Lord who is in
the temple, and ⁹ he who separates ¹⁰ the Word from the body
rejects the grace given us in it. And let not ¹¹ the most impious
Arians, because the body is a creature, suppose that ⌐the Word

---

¹ presumes B. ² Cf. *Num.*, *15, 30.* ³ for B. ⁴ church B. Cf. *Mt.*, *24, 2.* ⁵ nor
despising the temple did they go away and worship B. ⁶ not A. ⁷ which *om.* A.
⁸ He was stretched out A. ⁹ and *om.* B. ¹⁰ separated B. ¹¹ not *om.* B.

also is a creature [1], nor because the Word is not a creature slander
his body. For their evil mind is to be wondered at, since everything
they say is vain and confused, and they think up excuses only to
count the Creator with the creatures [2]. But let them listen : if the
5 Word is a creature, He would not have assumed a created body to
give it life. For what support ⌐would there be [3] to creation from a
creature when it also lacked salvation? But because, since the
Word is Creator [4], He was the maker of the creatures, therefore
at the end of the ages He put on what was created, that He might
10 be able again as Creator to renew and recreate it. But a creature
would never have been saved by a creature, as also creatures would
not have been created by a creature, unless the Word was the Creator.
So let them not falsify the divine Scriptures nor cause those
who are weak among the brethren to stumble. But if they wish,
15 let them also repent and no more serve creation instead of God
the Creator of all. But if they wish to persist in their impiety,
may they be alone in accepting these things and may they gnash
their teeth like their father the devil. For the faith of the Catholic
church knows God the Word as Creator of all and Maker, * and we *p. 51
20 know that in the beginning was the Word and the Word was with
God [5]. And we worship Him who also became man for our salvation,
not as the [6] equal who was incarnate in an equal body, but as the
Lord who took the form of a servant, and the Maker [7] and Creator
who was incarnate in [8] a creature, in order that in it ⌐having freed [9]
25 the whole world He might offer it to the Father and bring peace
to everything in heaven and earth. For so we recognise his divinity
as the Father's and we worship his coming in the flesh, even if
the mad Arians rend themselves.
Greet all those who love our Lord Jesus Christ [10].

The End.

---

[1] it is the Word B.   [2] creation B.   [3] was there A.   [4] of the creator B.   [5] *Jn.*, 1, *1*.
[6] an A.   [7] the Maker *om.* B.   [8] and B.   [9] He might free A.   [10] + for ever. Amen.B.

INDEX OF BIBLICAL QUOTATIONS

For the Old Testament the numbering of the Septuagint has been followed.   Direct quotations are marked with an asterisk.   References are to the pages of the English text.

Genesis

I, 1 : 7*, 11*
  27 : 11*
III, 19 : 32*

Exodus

III, 14 : 17*
IV, 11 : 11*
VIII, 19 : 12
XII, 41 : 19*
XV, 11 : 20*
XXI, 17 : 15*
XXXII, 4 : 7*
  34 : 7*

Leviticus

XXVI, 12 : 25

Numbers

XV, 30 : 40

Deuteronomy

XXXII, 17 : 9

Psalms

XIII, 1 : 17*
XXXV, 10 : 19*
XLII, 3 : 39*
XLV, 8 : 19*
LXXIV, 9 : 29
LXXXI, 5 : 35*
LXXXII, 2 : 20*
LXXXV, 8 : 20*

LXXXVIII, 49 : 33*
CV, 20 : 7*
CXXV, 6 : 13*
CXXXI, 14 : 25*
CXXXII, 1 : 25*

Proverbs

XXII, 28 : 14*

Joel

II, 25 : 19
III, 18 : 19*

Habakkuk

II, 15 : 29

Zechariah

XIII, 1 : 19*

Isaiah

VII, 14 : 39*
VIII, 14 : 18
XXVIII, 16 : 18
XXXII, 6 : 36*
LX, 1 : 19*

Jeremiah

II, 13 : 16*
IX, 9 : 17*
XXIII, 18 : 17*
  22 : 17*

Lamentations

II, 13 : 12

Daniel (Bel)

XIV, 5 : 11*

Matthew

I, 23 : 39*
V, 48 : 20*
VIII, 2 : 37*
X, 25 : 8*
XI, 28 : 12*
XII, 24 : 12
  24-28 : 1
  31-32 : 1
  32 : 12*
XIII, 54 : 8*
  55 : 6*
XV, 13 : 15*
XXIV, 2 : 40
XXV, 46 : 13*
XXVII, 40 : 31*
  42 : 6*

Mark

I, 40 : 37*
III, 29-30 : 8*
XV, 30 : 31*

Luke

V, 12 : 37*
VI, 36 : 20*
XI, 15 : 12
  19-20 : 10*
XIX, 42 : 7*

John

I, 1 : 5*, 12*, 41*
   3 : 3, 17*
   9 : 19*
  14 : 5*, 12*, 18*, 33*,
     36*, 36
v, 19 : 21
vi, 30 : 6*
  61-63 : 9*
vii, 15 : 6*
viii, 40 : 5*, 32*
  57 : 8*
ix, 32-33 : 8*
x, 21 : 9*
  30 : 5*, 19*, 20*, 21*,
    23*
  33 : 12*, 32*, 36
  35 : 21*
xi, 34 : 29*
xiii, 13 : 32*
xiv, 6 : 12*
  9 : 20*, 21*, 23*
  11 : 5*
xvi, 12-13 : 2*
  15 : 21*
xvii, 24 : 39*

Acts

I, 11 : 38*

Romans

I, 28 : 37
viii, 37 : 38*
  29 : 28
ix, 33 : 18

I Corinthians

I, 24 : 18*
viii, 6 : 18*
xi, 2 : 24*

II Corinthians

II, 8 : 4
iv, 11 : 19*
v, 17-18 : 18*
vi, 16 : 25*

Galatians

iv, 19 : 4*

Ephesians

iv, 5 : 4*, 25*

Philippians

II, 6-8 : 5*
  10-11 : 37*

Colossians

I, 16 : 17*
  17 : 3*

Titus

II, 13-14 : 39*
III, 10-11 : 31*, 36*

Hebrews

I, 3 : 17*, 18*, 19*
vi, 4-6 : 2*
ix, 10 : 4

James

I, 17 : 22*

I Peter

iv, 1 : 29*, 39*

II Peter

I, 4 : 38

INDEX OF PLACE NAMES AND PROPER NAMES

Aaron : 7, *26*.

Abraham : 8, *5*; 28, *33, 34*.

Adam : 20, *31*.

Adelphus : 35, *1, 2*.

Africa : 14, *1*.

Alexandria : 13, *10*; 25, *2*; 29, *32*.

Angels : 20, *30*; 38, *34*.

Anomoeans : 20, *18*.

Antioch : 23, *33*.

Apostle (Paul) : 4, *16, 24*; 23, *36*; 31, *26*; 36, *12*. Apostolic man (John Evangelist) : 5, *35*.

Arabia : 14, *15*.

Arian heresy : 14, *8, 27*; 15, *6, 26*; 17, *1*; 19, *32*; 22, *29*; 23, *22*; 26, *7, 10, 14*.

Arians : 12, *12, 14*; 14, *17, 31*; 17, *28*; 18, *14*; 19, *13*; 25, *8, 13*; 26, *3*; 27, *12*; 34, *15*; 36, *23*; 37, *19, 33*; 40, *9, 34*; 41, *28*.

Ariminum : 14, *25*; 15, *34, 36*; 16, *11, 12, 41, 25, 30*; 17, *7, 22, 36*; 20, *1*; 21, *5*; 22, *16*; 23, *31*.

Arius : 14, *30*; 15, *31*; 28, *10*.

Asterius : 25, *9, 22, 28*; 29, *33*.

Athanasius : 1, *1*; 13, *10*; 14, *1*; 24, *18*; 25, *12*; 30, *7*; 31, *1*; 35, *1, 3*.

Auxentius : 14, *17*; 16, *15*; 23, *21*.

Barbarians : 15, *11*.

Basilides : 26, *16*; 28, *11*.

Beelzebub (cf. Devil) : 1, *19*; 4, *11*; 6, *27*; 7, *4, 7, 11, 29*; 8, *7, 13*; 9, *13, 16, 18*; 10, *13, 21, 26*; 11, *5, 8, 11, 22, 25*; 12, *6, 14*.

Bishop(s) : 1, *2*; 14, *1, 3*; 16, *19, 32*; 18, *13, 28, 36*; 19, *13, 26, 34*; 20, *6*; 22, *18, 22*; 23, *17, 20*.

Caesarea (in Palestine) : 19, *31*.

Caiaphas : 31, *15*; 39, *30*.

Catechumens : 2, *17, 19*.

Centurion : 32, *11*.

Cherubim : 40, *3*.

Christian(s) : 15, *11*; 17, *28*; 22, *20*; 24, *11*; 31, *31*; 39, *6*.

Church : 6, *3*; 23, *21, 25*; 25, *5, 31*. Catholic church : 22, *35*; 23, *15, 29*; 24, *10*; 26, *19*; 41, *18*. Old church (Antioch) : 26, *2, 23, 27*.

Cilicia : 15, *27*.

Constantine : 16, *23, 25*.

Constantinople : 23, *32*.

Corinth : 4, *17*. Corinthians : 4, *17*.

Crete : 14, *13*.

Cyprus : 14, *13*.

Cyrus : 11, *15*.

Dalmatia : 14, *12*.

Damasus : 14, *3*; 23, *20*.

Daniel : 11, *15*.

Dardania : 14, *12*.

David : 33, *1*.

Demophilus : 16, *16*.

Devil (cf. Beelzebub) : 6, *17, 19, 29*; 7, *8*; 8, *25*; 11, *33*; 35, *7, 11, 31*; 39, *23*; 41, *18*.

Disciples (Apostles) : 7, *36*; 8, *12*; 32, *4, 7*; 38, *35*.

Easter : 15, *26*.

Egypt : 7, *15, 18*; 14, *14*; 19, *8*; 23, *16*; 25, *21*; 33, *26, 27*.

Emmanuel : 39, *13*.

Epirus : 14, *12*.

Eudoxus : 16, *15*.

Eusebians : 18, *20*; 19, *3*.

Eusebius (of Caesarea) : 19, *31*; (of Egypt) : 25, *9, 22, 27*; 29, *33*.

Exodus : 17, *11*.

Fathers (of the church) : 14, *6*; 15, *1, 35*; 19, *27*; 20, *8*; 22, *11, 15, 19, 22, 32*; 23, *34, 35*; 24, *6*; 26, *8*; 27, *1*; 28, *15*; 39, *10*.

Gabriel : 40, *23*.
Galatians : 4, *18*.
Gaul : 14, *4*.
Gentiles : 31, *28, 30*.
Gospel : 1, *2, 4*; 13, *6*.
Gregory : 23, *24*.

Heathen : 2, *17, 19*; 10, *28*; 12, *10*; 36, *23*; 39, *7*.
Heaven : 10, *3, 6*; 24, *15*; 37, *30*; 38, *22, 24, 34*; 40, *30*; 41, *26*.
Hebrews : 2, *8*; 4, *25, 27*; 17, *18*.
Hellas : 14, *12*.
Heresy (except Arian) : 24, *5*; 34, *14*; 35, *15*; 40, 9.
Heretic(s) (except Arians) : 27, *17*; 31, *26*; 36, *13*.

Indians : 15, *10*.
Isaiah : 10, *33*.
Isauria : 14, *14*; 23, *32*.
Israel : 40, *1*.
Italy : 14, *4*.

James : 22, *2*.
Jeremiah : 16, *7*; 17, *11, 15*.
Jerusalem : 40, *2*.
Jews : 5, *19*; 6, *21, 22*; 8, *15*; 12, *13*; 15, *28*; 16, *5*; 31, *11, 23, 29*; 32, *23*; 35, *11*; 36, *33*; 39, *7*.   New Jews : 34, *1*.
John (Baptist) : 3, *29*; (Evangelist) : 5, *7*; 9, *27*; 18, *19*.
Judas : 39, *29*.

Lazarus : 28, *34*; 29, *1*; 33, *11*; 40, *27*.
Libya : 14, *14*; 23, *16*.
Lycia : 14, *14*.

Macedonia : 14, *12*.
Magi : 33, *25*.
Magicians : 11, *36*; 12, *11*.

Mani : 28, *12*; 33, *19*.
Manichaeans : 26, *16*; 36, *2, 8*.
Marcion : 33, *19*; 36, *2*.
Marcionites : 36, *8*.
Mark : 8, *28*.
Mary (Mother of our Lord) : 28, *23*; 32, *20, 29*; 34, *5*.
Maximus : 31, *1*; 34, *19*.
Mediolanum : 23, *21*.
Mesopotamia : 15, *27*.
Moses : 11, *14*; 12, *1*.

Nicaea : 14, *20, 29*; 15, *4, 19, 20, 22, 24, 31*; 16, *12, 17, 21, 33*; 17, *4, 10, 24*; 18, *2*; 19, *33*; 20, *2, 6*; 22, *17*; 23, *34*; 24, *4*; 26, *8, 12, 29, 34*; 27, *2, 4, 11*; 28, *14*; 29, *20, 29*; 34, *13*.
Ninevites : 12, 9.

Origen : 2, *1, 13*.

Pamphylia : 14, *13*.
Paul (Apostle) : 2, *6*; 5, *8*; 17, *17*; 18, *20*; 39, *17*; (of Samosata) : 26, *15*; 28, *10*; 33, *23*.
Paulinus : 26, *6, 28*.
Peter : 7, *1*; 29, *5*; 38, *8*; 39, *16*.
Pharaoh : 11, *36*; 12, *11*.
Pharisees : 1, *17*; 2, *25, 33, 34*; 6, *14, 22, 27*; 7, *3, 27*; 8, *3, 27*; 9, *3*; 10, *11*; 11, *18*; 12, *3, 17*.
Pilate : 31, *10*.   Pilate's wife : 31, *12*.
Prince (Devil) : 40, *29*.
Prophet (Isaiah) : 11, *3*; 36, *15*.   Prophets: 32, *16*; 39, 11.
Psalmist : 25, *15*.
Psalms : 13, *6*.

Rome : 14, *3*; 19, *29*; 23, *20, 27*.

Sabellius : 26, *15*; 27, *33*; 28, *10*.
Saint (Psalmist) : 20, *33*.   Saints : 32, *17*.
Sardica : 26, *31, 36*.
Scribes : 12, *3*.
Scripture(s) : 5, *6*; 7, *26*; 11, *26*; 17, *10, 20*; 19, *14, 20, 21*; 21, *18*; 32, *21*; 41, *13*.

Sheol : 33, *3*.
Shepherd (Hermas) : 18, *25*.
Sicily : 14, *13*.
Simon : 5, *28*.
Sirmium : 23, *31*.
Sodomites : 12, *9*.
Son of Man : 9, *21, 30*; 10, *3, 9*.
Stephen : 38, *33*.
Syria : 15, *27*.

Temple (in Jerusalem): 40, *3, 11, 13, 17, 19, 21*; (Lord's body) : 40, *12, 18, 25, 31, 32*.
Testaments : 39, *11*.
Theognostus : 2, *2, 26*.

Thomas : 32, *2*.
Thrace : 16, *28, 35*; 23, *32*.
Trinity : 3, *13, 23*; 24, *9, 13*; 26, *11*; 27, *22, 27*.

Ursacius : 14, *17*; 16, *14*; 23, *27*.

Valens : 16, *15*.
Valentinians : 36, *8*.
Valentinus : 14, *18*; 23, *27*; 26, *16*; 28, *11*; 36, *2*.

Zion : 18, *6*.

TABLE OF CONTENTS

Introduction   I
Translations

    Ad Serapionem IV   1
    Ad Afros   14
    Ad Antiochenos   25
    Ad Maximum   31
    Ad Adelphium   35

Index of Biblical Quotations   43
Index of Place Names and Proper Names   45
Table of Contents   49

Imprimerie Orientaliste, S.P.R.L., Louvain (Belgique)

D 1967/0602/14